THE WAY IT WAS

A HISTORY OF THE OXFORDSHIRE COTSWOLDS IN OLD PHOTOGRAPHIC POSTCARDS

DEREK JAMES BASON
GREGORY LEE BASON

PUBLISHING

First published in Great Britain byThe Breedon Books Publishing Company Limited
Breedon House, 44 Friar Gate, Derby, DE1 1DA. 1999

This paperback edition published in Great Britain in 2015 by DB Publishing, an imprint of
JMD Media Ltd

ISBN 978-1-78091-485-5

Printed and bound in the UK by Copytech (UK) Ltd Peterborough

THE WAY IT WAS

For my father, Derek James Bason

Acknowledgements

My father's love of local history and collecting old postcards and photographs resulted in the original idea for *The Way It Was* in the early 1980s.

Following my father's death in 1986, *The Way It Was* lay unfinished for many years until, in January 1998, I determined to complete his work. At that time it consisted of about 60 postcards arranged into six chapters. Over the last two years I have added around 50 postcards and captions, while keeping the overall structure of the book the same.

Over the years many people and organisations, both local and national, have contributed towards *The Way It Was*. Museums, libraries, local people, friends, and family have supplied valuable information, kindly lent postcards, and shared their memories. Without their help this book would not have been possible. But my greatest thanks go to my sister for her thoughtful suggestions and patient proofreading, and to my mother and my fiancée for their support and encouragement.

Contents

Introduction

T HE 20TH CENTURY saw some of the most dramatic changes in the history of humankind. We moved from an age when the letter and postcard were the only means of keeping in touch, to an age when people regularly communicated with each other all over the world via telephones, computers, and satellites. The century began with the bicycle, horse, and steam locomotive as the main methods of transport, and ended in an era of private car ownership and relatively inexpensive international travel. The nature of work also continued to change as traditional manufacturing declined and agriculture responded to a more competitive and global marketplace. This shift towards employment in the service industries, and tourism in particular, is sure to continue in the 21st century. Many traditional rural recreations and pastimes have disappeared or been adapted for modern times. New leisure pursuits have arisen that would have been impossible to imagine when our grandparents were young.

There can be no doubt that, since the turn of the last century, English life has changed forever. The quiet, unhurried, and more communal way of life depicted by the postcards in this book has all but disappeared. The village itself no longer exists in glorious isolation, and our towns are noisier, less gentle, and less distinct in personality. However, while possibly lamenting such changes, we should be wary of wishing to return to the 'good old days', for then there was much hardship and fewer opportunities. Advances in health, education, and technology have led to greatly increased levels of personal freedom and opportunity, and I ask the reader to bear this in mind as they read this book.

The geographical region covered by *The Way It Was* could loosely be described as the Oxfordshire Cotswolds and surrounding area. That is, the region from Banbury in the north to Witney in the south, and from Middleton Stoney in the east to the border with Gloucestershire and Warwickshire in the west. Although Oxfordshire was not intended to be a distinct unit when its borders were laid out in about 1010, the area covered by this book has always been characterised and influenced by the Cotswold Hills, which in places rise to over 700 feet. The hills are good for sheep grazing, and in the Middle Ages the Cotswold wool trade brought much wealth to the towns of Witney, Burford, and Chipping Norton.

The towns and villages in this region contain many fine buildings that bear witness to an opulent past. The characteristic building material in this area is grey limestone and Stonesfield slate. In the north of the county, in the neighbourhood of Banbury, the limestone changes to a golden-brown colour due to iron deposits. It is from this ironstone that many pretty villages were built; Wroxton, Bloxham, Horley, and Hornton are but a few examples.

The Way It Was primarily covers the period from the turn of the century to the eve of World War Two, with some references to earlier and later times. Although not presented in chronological order, the book takes us from the Edwardian Golden Age, through the horrors of World War One, and on to the dramatic changes of the 1920s and 1930s. It is the effects of the Great War and the rapid advances in transportation and communications that make this period of our social history such an interesting area for study.

I hope that this pictorial social history of north-west Oxfordshire will attract readers of all ages. The eldest will be reminded of people, places, and events from their childhood, while the youngest can learn a little about the world of their parents or grandparents. Whatever their age, it is surely with fascination and perhaps with a little foreboding that they will consider how everyday life may change in the first 100 years of the new millennium.

Gregory Lee Bason
Long Hanborough, Oxfordshire.
January 2000

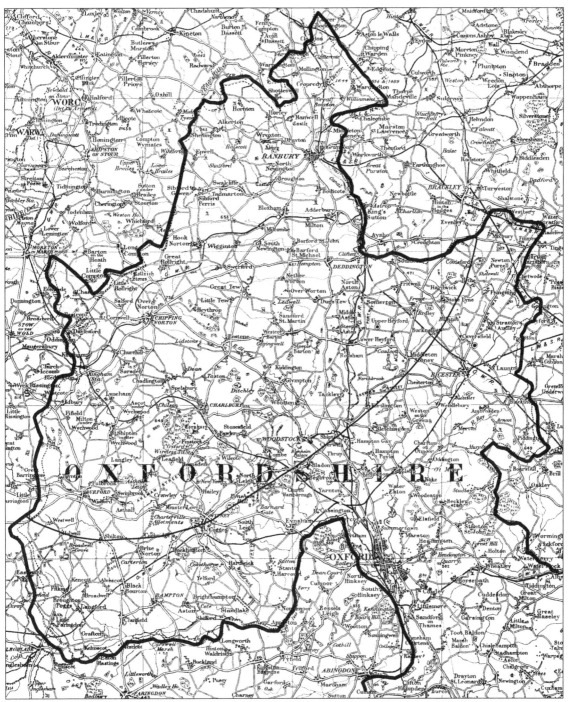

A map of central and north Oxfordshire, showing the county border prior to the county boundary changes of 1974. The area covered by this book lies north of the thin black line that runs across the centre of the county.

Chapter One
The Rural Scene

Cropredy. A sunny day as a horse and cart slowly makes its way up the lane to Williamscot in the mid 1920s. Cropredy is one of the most northern villages in the county. The Church of St Mary, built in 1320, houses a suit of armour discovered on the site of the Battle of Cropredy Bridge, which took place in 1644 during the Civil War.

Burdrop. A typical small Oxfordshire village as it was in 1910. The sender, who wrote the postcard on 22 July 1910, says: 'Here it is stormy, warm, cold, hot, windy, wet, brilliant sunshine, etc. etc., all in a day, most trying for haymaking.'

Barford St Michael. A quiet corner, yet a village full of life. Typically, on May Day the children would go around the village looking very gay and bright, bedecked with flowers and carrying Union Jacks. Cricket matches and fireworks often featured in May Day celebrations.

Thatched cottages, Milcombe. The doorways to these mellowed stone and thatched cottages are reached by walking up the narrow brick path, past a border of typical cottage garden flowers. Notice the wood leaning against a shed, drying out ready for the open fire.

Ploughing match. These matches were a regular feature in the agricultural calendar, so much so that some ploughmen had a match plough that was only used at these events. A single plough pulled by two horses is pictured here; a double plough would have used three horses.

Minster Lovell. A tranquil street scene photographed before the arrival of the telephone and television. A channel runs alongside the road helping to guide rainwater into the nearby River Windrush during wet weather. Wooden bridges providing accesss to the enchanting cottages complete this delightful scene.

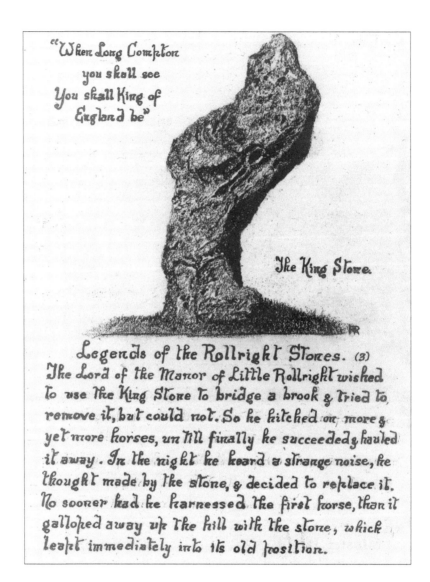

"When Long Compton
you shall see
You shall King of
England be"

The King Stone.

Legends of the Rollright Stones. (3)
The Lord of the Manor of Little Rollright wished
to use the King Stone to bridge a brook & tried to
remove it, but could not. So he hitched on more &
yet more horses, un till finally he succeeded & hauled
it away. In the night he heard a strange noise, he
thought made by the stone, & decided to replace it.
No sooner had he harnessed the first horse, than it
galloped away up the hill with the stone, which
leapt immediately into its old position.

Rollright Stones. These stones have been part of the
Oxfordshire landscape for thousands of years. Generations
treading the path around the stone circle have wondered at the
four stones called the Whispering Knights. Sometimes
overlooked, but equally part of this ancient scene, is the solitary
King's Stone, 100 paces north of the circle. It stands some eight
feet tall on a 700 foot high ridge.

Middleton Stoney. A rural village that looks deceptively deserted, but in fact was a place of daylong activity. Early morning would see domestic servants and gardeners hurrying to Middleton Park, and boys from the age of 13 setting out to do a day's work on the farm. The older folk would be making rugs, sawing wood, fetching water, and making jam, yet still finding time to tend the garden.

The Grange Gardens, Ascott-under-Wychwood.
A peaceful retreat. The sender of this card agrees as
she writes, 'We are here for the rest cure, it is a treat
to do just as we like but the time will go too quickly.'
Posted at Ascott-under-Wychwood on 16 July 1913.

Fritwell. This rural farm scene of unmade roads, iron railings, and chickens free to roam was photographed sometime before 1913, when the first autumn leaves were beginning to fall.

The vegetable garden. This photograph was taken during an era when you went without if you did not grow it yourself. It was hard to find the money for seeds and plants, and seed was always kept from the previous year's harvest. To actually buy a 'score' of plants was very rare. A well-stocked garden was essential, and while country folk might not have been educated, they were rich in the knowledge of soil, weather, and accurate planting times. It took experience and skill to produce food from a garden every week throughout the year.

Salford. This superb old photograph was taken in 1908. It gives an insight into working-class folk; characters of a bygone age. This was a village gath - ering, a time to join together in sharing a social life, but the photograph clearly captures the individ - uality of the club members.

Sunday stroll. This young lad in his 'Sunday best' was probably out for a Sunday evening stroll with his parents when this photograph was taken. It shows him in a wheat field, in front of a 'stook' of corn (the name given to a method of stacking for drying). 'I want it well cut! Well bound! Well shocked!', would have been the traditional cry. A figure was sometimes made from twisted sheaves of the last corn to be cut. This was hung up and kept for good luck until the next year's harvest.

Hook Norton. Nature looks its best in the countryside, but when the elements are against you the effects can be quite dramatic. The villagers of Hook Norton discovered this when they woke up on Sunday, 22 September 1935 after the great hailstorm.

Cornwell, or Cornewelle as it was spelt in the *Domesday Book.* A village with a matured, rustic look with its established gardens enclosed by drystone walling, and cottage roofs either thatched, or clad in Stonesfield tiles.

Wroxton. Lord North and the Abbey have long been associated with Wroxton, so much so that this pretty, rural village, a community in its own right, could be overlooked. Careful study of the photograph shows the village post office and sundial next door to the forge, with its blacksmith in his leather apron. There are village folk in the street as well as a farmyard horse and cart and various animals. All these complete a scene of truly yesteryear.

Chapter Two
Somewhere to Live

Sibford Ferris. The village post office was also the family home. On the death of a village postmaster or postmistress the location of the post office moved to the home of the new village official.

Tadmarton. Tiny, newly thatched cottages with bread ovens, built of local stone. These were very often home to large families, mainly employed as labourers in agriculture or as domestic servants.

The Litchfield Arms, Enstone. This imposing old inn must have been home for many families over the years, but they may not all have lived at the Litchfield Arms since old inns had a habit of changing their signs. In the early 1800s, a change to a name including the word 'Arms' was quite common, but a really old inn would have been called the Fox or the Star. A picture sign would tell its name; after all it was for the benefit of a generation of people of whom very few could read.

'A bit of old Charlbury'. This photograph shows Armada
Cottage and the Old Talbot in Thames Street. These two
cottages, built from coursed rubble with stone slate roofs, were
probably built as a single house. A plaque outside Armada
Cottage dates the building from 1587. The Greyhound, or
Dog, became known as the Talbot in 1864 and kept the name
until its closure early in the 20th century.

Chastleton. A fine Jacobean house built and occupied by a wealthy wool merchant from Witney and his family. The house has a grand oak staircase, many elaborate rooms, and must have employed many servants below-stairs as was the custom in bygone days.

Deddington. In the early part of the 20th century, travellers leaving Deddington and heading south would have passed two well-known landmarks: Turnpike Cottage at the bottom of the hill, and the Fox and Crown public house at the top. The photograph shows Turnpike Cottage being demolished in about 1928. A Mr R. Kearsey had bought it for £50. He used the materials to build a bungalow along the Hempton Road.

Council houses. The building of council houses was widespread just after World War One. These were built at Wroxton around 1920 by Henry Boot of Sheffield. Many local tradesman were employed on the site, including the Price brothers from Drayton; Jack Palmer and son, bricklayers; Harry Gilkes, scaffolder; and Harry and Ernest Hancox, stonemasons. It is interesting to note the fashion: everyone is wearing either a cap or a trilby.

Gambon's Mill. This mill, which was recorded in the *Domesday Book* of 1086, is on the eastern edge of the parish of North Aston. The mill was held by the Gambon family for most of the 13th century, and was called Gambon's Mill until late in the 18th century. The double mill seems to have been in use from the late 16th century until the early 18th century. The Rose family were the millers from the middle of the 17th century until 1938. By 1955 the mill had been converted for private use, although restored machinery remained in the building until 1980.

Glympton. A pretty summer scene showing Glympton Vicarage and the River Glyme, around 1930. The Vicarage belonged to the Oxford Diocese until 1961, before being sold to a private buyer, Dr Graham Swift, who lived there until 1995. The house now belongs to the Glympton Park Estate.

Milton. Joseph George Bennett, born in 1870, was the seventh child of a master shoemaker. He and his wife, Elizabeth Mary, had eight children, all born and brought up in this thatched cottage with its distinctive 14th-century doorway. One of the children was Mr Arthur Bennett, who would often recall his early childhood and how they managed with just three bedrooms.

Almshouses are mediaeval in origin. Built to provide accommodation for the aged or needy, they were founded by religious guilds or local benefactors, and were therefore distinct from publicly financed poorhouses or workhouses.

Burford almshouses. The almshouses in Burford were built between 1456 and 1476, and claim Richard Earl of Warwick as their founder. However, the true founder is said to have been Henry Bishop, who gave money to build almshouses for the poor of the town. Bishop only received permission from the Lord of the Manor to endow them on condition that the Earl and Countess of Warwick were named as founders. The almshouses are shown here as they were in the 1930s.

Chipping Norton almshouses. Many more almshouses were founded in the 17th century. Those at Chipping Norton were established in 1640 by Henry Cornish for eight poor widows of the town. The inscription above the arch reads 'Remember the Poor'.

Shipton Court, Shipton-under-Wychwood. Now divided into residential flats, this beautiful Elizabethan building was built by the Lacys in 1603. It is said to be haunted by the ghost of Sir John Chandos Reade. Sir John, who owned the house in the mid-19th century, was an alcoholic who used to drink regularly with his butler. One evening the butler tried to ring for some more bottles, but Sir John, affected by the carousal, threw the bell rope over a picture. When the butler attempted to recover the rope he slipped and was impaled on a firedog. Although the question of whether the butler slipped or was pushed was raised, a verdict of accidental death was recorded. Nevertheless, Sir John never went drinking again and died a disturbed man in 1868. His ghost has often been seen since, despite the efforts of an exorcist.

Shipton-under-Wychwood. Two pretty cottages photographed around 1913. Alfred Miles, cabinet-maker and undertaker, lived in the cottage on the left for many years. His workshop was along the Ascott Road, past the gas works. Frank Coombes lived on the right. He was a well-known local man who began working for Alfred Willis' saddlery business after leaving school. Apart from service in World War One, Mr Coombes stayed with the firm all his life and finally took it over after the death of Alfred Willis in 1949.

The ancient market town of Burford, known as the 'gateway to the Cotswolds', grew rich in the Middle Ages from the Cotswold wool trade. To this day many beautiful stone houses bear witness to the town's opulent past.

The Old Rectory House, Priory Lane, Burford. This house, together with the nearby priory, was held by the Lenthall family for about 200 years. Since 1949 the building has been used as a guest house by the community.

Burford Priory. Burford Priory is a fine old house with a history interwoven with the Harman, Tanfield, and Lenthall families. The house has undergone many changes over the centuries, and it is likely that this photograph was taken during the period of restoration work carried out by Mr Horniman, owner of the Priory from 1912 to 1932. Today, the Priory is used as a convent and is closed to the public.

Westhall Hill. Just outside Burford lies the small village of Westhall Hill, with its graceful four-gabled manor house. It is likely to have been the Bartholomews, owners of the house for most of the 17th century, who altered and enlarged the building to give it the appearance it has today.

Chapter Three
A Job of Work

Mark Quartermain. A carter who died in 1943, aged 87, after spending a lifetime with working horses. He was a true Oxfordshire man bearing an old Oxfordshire name dating back to Herbert and Robertus Quartermain, who lived in Merton in 1187.

James Robins. A ploughman and winner of many prizes at the Banbury Agricultural Association meetings. He is seen here toiling away during a long hard day in the field. A break for bread and cheese or home-cured bacon, helped down with a bottle of cold tea without milk, was taken under the hedge. The day was not finished until his workmates had been unharnessed, fed, and watered.

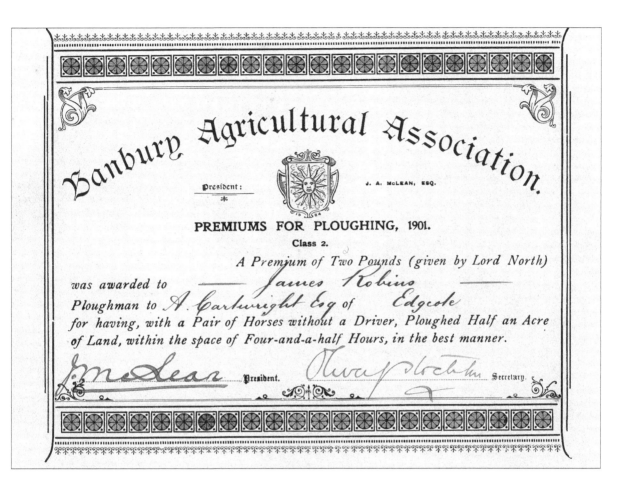

Award for ploughing. One of the many certificates awarded to James Robins.

Theodore Lamb. A true craftsman who wandered the lanes and villages of north Oxfordshire repairing clocks and watches, albeit to maintain only a poor standard of living. Although a clockmaker, he is best remembered by the locals as being a hermit who wore a sackcloth and rough home-made sandals and who lived in a shack at the side of the road. This photograph shows him paused by a heap of broken stones for road mending. His trolley was home-made and had a paraffin lantern on the front to light his way.

Village blacksmith. Charlie Coleman followed in his father's footsteps, sweating at the forge, hammering at the anvil, and shoeing horses. He is pictured here with his father Joseph, outside their blacksmith's shop in Adderbury.

Skilled farm worker, early 1920s. A farm worker mowing the meadow grass ready for making hay. After going through the hay press, the hay would be stacked, stored and then used as winter fodder. For working a 50 hour week this man would have been paid 28 shillings if he was over 21 and 25 shillings if he was under 21; 14-year-old boys would have been paid 8s 6d per week.

Industrial town. As Banbury changed from a market town to an industrial town the type of labour required began to change. Skilled workers in particular were now needed. In 1859 a Banbury branch of the Amalgamated Society of Engineers, Machinists, Millwrights, Smiths, and Pattern Makers was formed. The first recorded meeting was held from 8pm until 9.30pm on Saturday, 6 August 1859 at the Wheatsheaf public house, Banbury. A minute from the 20 August meeting reads, '...that a carpet bag will be supplyed [sic] to the Secretary for his use in carrying books etc. belonging to this branch from and to his home and that the branch defrays the expense.' On 11 February 1867, it was agreed that the secretary would write to the Executive Council concerning men working two lathes. The reply is dated 14 March 1867 and reads as follows, including a reference to funeral money:

Dear Sir

In answer to your letter concerning members working two lathes, I have to inform you that the Council entirely disapprove of such a system, and in the case you allude to the Council would recommend the Branch to instruct the member not to continue the practice, and in the event of him refusing to comply the Branch must exclude him from the society.

You must give him all the instructions by word of mouth, and thereby avoid having any written communication with him.

With regard to the funeral money of the late J.B. Bashnell, the Branch can pay the benefit for the parties named by J.L. Pratt, the Barrister appointed to certify the rules of savings banks, at the same time, if any one of them paid the funeral expenses that must be paid, to the extent of £5, to the party who paid the same, and then the balance £7 shared amongst them, including the one who may have paid the £5.

I am yours truly
W. Allan

Weaving factory. In this picture, taken in the early 20th century, the working women and working conditions in the huge factory room speak for themselves. The advent of power looms saw an end to weaving as a cottage industry that had been associated with the Witney area for over two centuries.

Early's of Witney, makers of fine blankets since 1669. This photograph shows Early's, the oldest blanket works in Witney, taken around 1909 from the River Windrush. Over the centuries the river has provided power for the weaving industry. What a peaceful contrast the riverside must have been from the noise and clamour of the weaving room.

Kingham. A fascinating picture of school life around 1913. Perhaps some of the people in the photograph are still alive today? What stories would they have to tell, and what did they achieve in life? Note the plants on the window ledge, the varnished roll-up pictures, and the two boys sitting with the girls, even though there is space elsewhere: this used to be a form of punishment.

T. E. Griffin, baker. In the centre of this tranquil village scene is the bread and delivery service of the day. Mr T. E. Griffin was a local baker who had his bakehouse at the side of the church at Epwell. Twice weekly he supplied the surrounding villages, including Sibford Gower where this photograph was taken. The superb stonework over the village well is the work of local stonemason, Mr Wilkes.

Man, machine and horse. Taken near Deddington around 1917, this old photograph marks a time in our history when man and machine took over from man and his horse, which had for so long sowed, reaped, and harvested the Oxfordshire countryside.

Harvest time. Taken deep in the heart of the Oxfordshire countryside at the onset of World War One, this was a familiar harvest-time scene. An old binder and early tractor are ready to reap a field of waving golden corn. Once the early sun had evaporated the morning dew, the days work could start and would not end until darkness fell. Weary workers and tired-out children would make their way home under a pale harvest moon.

On strike. In December 1913, Union members at Bliss Tweed Mill came out on a seven-month-long strike over wages and union recognition. They can be seen here marching through Chipping Norton with a banner that reads, 'We fight for liberty. Down with oppression.' Members of the strike committee were jailed at Oxford and included at least one woman. She was presented with a silver tea service by supporters on her release. Non-union workers did not want to strike, but because of the bitterness felt towards them, they had to be escorted to work by the local constabulary. It was a strike that divided the town and brought heartache to many families.

Loyal employees. A group of workers showing their intentions with a placard that reads, 'Bliss Loyal Employe's [sic].'

Deddington, around 1923. The young man second from the left is Mr Allen Course, who was born at nearby Deddington Mill. In 1932 the fire engine was housed at the town hall, which was convenient for the town well. It had previously been kept in a building on the Green.

Fire at Alfred Groves and Sons, Milton-under-Wychwood. As the photograph shows, a lot of damage was caused by the fire of 1926. Perhaps consolation would have been taken from the fact that at least the gantry's wooden structure seems to have survived intact. Notice the men to the right of the picture inspecting the debris, no doubt trying to decide what is fit for salvage. Alfred Groves and Sons Ltd., building contractors, are still in operation today, continuing a business established over 300 years ago.

Shutford. This picture of Shutford schoolgirls was taken in the early 1920s and, considering the size of the village, they must all have been present. Many probably ended up working at Wrenches thriving plush factory. One who did not was Miss Violet Turner, pictured here in the second row, fourth from the right. Instead, the young Miss Turner went into service after leaving school. The Turner family had long been associated with plush weaving in Shutford. Miss Violet Turner's father Alfred, her grandfather Amos, and her uncle William were all hand weavers at the factory.

Claydon post office. The photograph on the left shows the village post office before it moved to its new location shown on the right. The young lady on the right, outside the new post office building, is Mrs Annie Marie Prew. Born in 1889, she lived and worked at the post office during World War One. Then, as now, the Post Office was a large employer of both men and women. In 1914, around 123,000 people worked for the Post Office, accounting for over 70% of all Civil Service employment. Claydon village post office later returned to the original building. Today the sub-post office is housed in a modern building along the road to Boddington.

Banbury cattle market. This superb postcard was posted in May 1904. Cattle can be seen in front of the town hall, and by the footpath railings. Nearby, carrier's carts await the return home. Notice the crowd gathered outside the town hall for the auction. No doubt throughout the day many deals would be struck as well as news and gossip exchanged; this was an important community gathering. Cattle were sold in the streets of Banbury for the last time in 1931. The cattle market then moved from Cow Fair to purpose-built premises in Grimsbury.

The Tolsey in Burford High Street, around 1905. During the Middle Ages Burford was run by a Guild of Merchants who were entitled to hold a market and collect tolls from anyone wishing to trade in the town. It was the Guild of Merchants who built the Tolsey, or toll-house, sometime before 1561, as a place to hold meetings and receive tolls. In 1617 Sir Lawrence Tanfield bought the Lordship of the Manor and successfully took the Guild to court for usurping the rights of the Lord of the Manor. As a consequence, Tanfield became so unpopular that following his death in 1625, his effigy was burnt in the High Street every Midsummer's Day for 200 years.

Slatters and Olivers. In the mid 1920s, Long Hanborough boasted two garages: Slatters and Olivers. The latter was started in 1919 by Harry Oliver, with just one Model-T Ford. He is pictured here outside his garage with various vehicles for sale and hire. For many years the company also used the building opposite, previously the parish hall, as a workshop. The garage moved to its present position on the south side of Main Road in the mid 1960s. Today, John Oliver, son of Harry, continues the family business.

Chipping Norton Red Cross Hospital. Taken during World War One, when cameras were far from commonplace, this lasting record of social history was the work of the Chipping Norton photographer Mr Frank Packer. Many old Oxfordshire scenes would be lost forever, or exist only in fading memories, if it had not been for the work of local photographers such as Percy Simms, Frank Packer, and later his son Basil Packer. The present-day local historian owes much to the work of such men.

Chapter Four

Transport

Steam railways. Very few aspects of life were left untouched by the coming of the railways and steam locomotion. Heavy goods could now be carried long distances at speed, and people could cross the country in hours instead of days. In the 1920s, even cross country lines like this one at Chipping Norton were busy places, with supplies being brought in for the town and nearly all the visitors, post and cattle travelling by rail. Horse-drawn drays were used to haul deliveries up New Street to the town centre. The line from Chipping Norton to Kings Sutton closed to passengers in June 1951; the Great Western line from Kingham to Chipping Norton closed to all traffic in December 1962.

Great Western, London and North Western Railway station. Banbury, about 1854. During World War One the station, although short of staff, handled many troop trains. In February 1915, upwards of 12,000 of the London NW Company's staff had responded to the nation's call, as well as some 10,000 of the Great Western staff.

Copyright Reg. No. 58330.   INSURANCE POST CARD SERIES   Copyright Reg. No. 58330.

POST CARD

INSURANCE.

THE OCEAN ACCIDENT & GUARANTEE COR-PORATION LIMITED (Principal Office: Moorgate Street, London, E.C.; Chief Office for Australia: 131, Pitt Street, Sydney, N.S.W.; Chief Office for New Zealand: 4, Customhouse Quay, Wellington; Chief Office for South Africa: Fletcher's Chambers, Darling Street, Cape Town) insures the *bona fide* holder of this postcard (being the person to whom it is addressed) in the sum of **£50** in case of death caused by an accident within the United Kingdom, Australia, New Zealand, or British South Africa, to any passenger-train, public omnibus (motor or horse), tramcar, or four-wheeled or hansom cab (driven by a licensed driver plying for public hire), in which such holder is travelling as an ordinary ticket-bearing or fare-paying passenger.

PROVIDED that the above undertaking is subject to the following special conditions, which are of the essence of the contract, viz. :— (a) That death result within thirty days after the accident; (b) that such holder shall, prior to the accident, have written his (or her) usual signature in ink in the space provided underneath; (c) that notice of the accident be given to the Corporation at its Principal Office in London within fourteen days after its occurrence if in the United Kingdom, or within a reasonable time after its occurrence if elsewhere; and (d) that this Insurance applies only to persons over twelve and under seventy years of age, is limited to one Insurance for any one holder, and holds good for seven days only from the time printed by the Post Office cancelling stamp, expiring in any event, however, on December 31st, 1909.

This Insurance entitles the holder to the benefit of, and is subject to, the conditions of the " Ocean Accident and Guarantee Company Limited, Act, 1890," Risks Nos. 2 and 3, when they are not incompatible with the special conditions above stated.

No. 601,093.

Signature of holder..

You may write across the Coupon.

Copyright Reg. No. 58330.

INSURANCE.

STAMP.

Printed in Saxony.

ADDRESS SIDE.

Insurance policy. The reverse side of a postcard of Oxfordshire that acted as an insurance policy should the purchaser die as a result of an accident caused by a passenger train, public omnibus (motor or horse), tramcar, or other form of public transport. The insurance was valid on purchase of the postcard, and covered seven days from the date of the Post Office cancelling stamp. This particular postcard was valid for the year 1909.

Carrier's carts. During Victorian and Edwardian times, carrier's carts provided a vital means of transportation and communication between villages and towns. North Oxfordshire was no exception, with the people of Banburyshire making regular use of carrier's carts to travel to Banbury to exchange goods and news. One of the many carriers was William Gregory Bason, pictured here in 1908 outside St Mary's church in Banbury. William Bason's regular service connected Milton, Adderbury, and Banbury.

Pony and Trap. What better way to illustrate the pace of life than this postcard, posted in 1912. It was a long, hot summer that year, as indicated by the dry mud bank and confirmed by the resident of No. 14, Taynton who wrote, 'I expect you know what view this is, its the bridge round the old way. We are having it very hot now, makes work go hard. Father said he's been over that bridge many a time.'

Miss Susie Tustain. Newspapers of the day carried adverts depicting young ladies in pretty clothes riding bicycles, encouraging women to take up cycling as a hobby. But in real rural areas the bicycle was a way of life, not a hobby, whether used to post a letter, visit the vicar, or fetch the doctor. When Miss Susie Tustain was more than three score years and ten she would often reflect, 'What would I have done without the bike?'

PICTURE

Meeting of the four shires. This monument marks the meeting of the four shires: Oxfordshire, Warwickshire, Worcestershire, and Gloucestershire. The stone can still be seen today, situated about six miles north-west of Chipping Norton on the A44. However, as a result of county boundary changes, it no longer marks the meeting of the four shires.

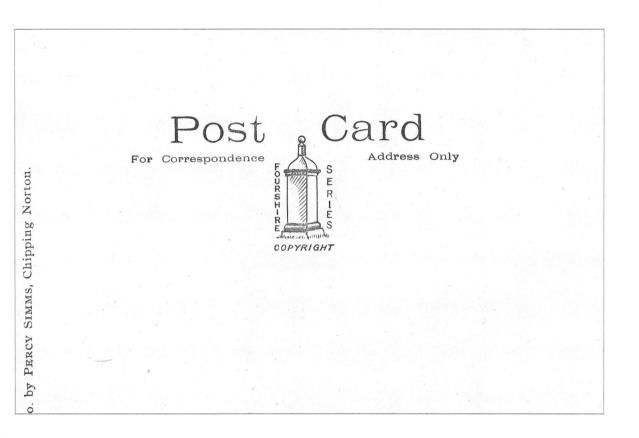

Four shires postcards. A series of postcards depicting scenes from the four shires was produced by Percy Simms between the late 1920s and the early 1930s. Each one had the four shires logo printed on the back.

A bright cold morning. This is 1916, the third winter into World War One, and the local men have been busy clearing nature's work. Snow was a much longed for event among the children, as much then as it is today, especially if it meant a morning off school because of blocked roads. However, the little chap on the left seems to have had enough and is probably thinking of his warm home and mum's cooking.

Chipping Norton crossroads. This photograph was taken on a clear, tranquil summer's day sometime before 1918. The faithful horse had been the main form of local transport for many centuries, but soon the first motor vehicles would be regularly disturbing these graceful, tree-lined tracks and roads. From this point, traders could travel north-east to Banbury cattle market, later to become the largest in Europe, or south-east to Oxford, passing through Enstone and Woodstock along the way.

Bletchingdon crossroads. This postcard shows the main road to Hampton Poyle and Oxford. The Red Lion public house to the left of the picture must have been a welcome retreat for the commercial traveller. It would have provided a break from the hot dusty road, and a chance to exchange news and gossip over some much deserved liquid refreshment. The Halls public house was run by the Barratt sisters until the early 1950s. Today the building is a private house.

Witney High Street. Close inspection of this charming postcard reveals some of the numerous ways in which people and goods were carried in the first decade of the 20th century. The solidly built horse-drawn dray, ironically pictured here outside a temperance hotel, belonged to Hitchman's brewery, a long-established Chipping Norton company. With branches in Worcester, Stratford-upon-Avon, Warwick, Blockley, Evesham, and Oxford, Hitchman's drays must have been a common sight gently winding their way along the county's roads. Hitchman's brewery closed in 1932, having been a major employer in Chipping Norton since 1796.

Charlbury toll house. During the 17th century the increase in popularity of coach transport began to seriously affect the county's road network. Many roads were little more than rough tracks and could not withstand the increased wear and tear. In an attempt to organise road repair, turnpike trusts were set up. The trusts financed road repair by raising money from tolls. The first turnpike trust in Oxfordshire was set up in 1718, and covered the London road from Oxford to Stokenchurch. The road from Charlbury to Witney was turnpiked in 1800. The growth of the railways in the 19th century caused a decline in coach travel, and by around 1878 most turnpike trusts had run out of funds and were disbanded. Tollhouses were usually round or octagonal so that the keeper had windows facing up and down the road as well as towards the gate.

Banbury Cross and St Mary's church. This photograph is likely to have been taken in the early to mid 1920s. The relatively new-looking statues of Queen Victoria, Edward VII, and George V were installed in 1914 to mark the coronation of George V in 1911. In 1888 the cross was redecorated, new gaslights were installed, and iron railings erected. These were removed in 1927. The general layout of this part of Banbury has not changed significantly since the photograph was taken. Today however, it would be difficult to capture such a quiet scene, with its uncrowded roads and solitary Midland Red bus.

Burford High Street. This photograph was clearly taken at an age when the motor vehicle had started to dominate the town's main streets. Notice the six motor cars, a motorcycle, a motorcycle with sidecar, and a public motorbus as well as various items of street furniture.

Chipping Norton High Street, around 1908. In this rare photographic postcard it looks as if the whole town has stopped their daily business to come and look at an electric light standard that has been knocked over by a motor car. For the moment however, the townsfolk's interest seems to lie more in the opportunity to be in a photograph than with the fallen light.

Charabanc. Originating in France and literally meaning 'wagon with benches', charabancs became a popular form of motor transport following World War One. This photograph was taken in Chipping Norton during a parish church Bible class outing to Windsor. What an experience it must have been for the women on board. They certainly seem in high spirits on what appears to be a glorious summer's day. Notice the large hood at the back of the vehicle however, which acted as a safeguard lest the weather should turn.

Motorcycle and side-car. This photograph, taken around 1926, shows Rose Trinder and her daughter Joan next to a BSA (Birmingham Small Arms) Big Twin motorcycle and sidecar combination. Such vehicles were used extensively throughout the 1920s, when the cost of purchasing even a small private motor car was prohibitive to the vast majority of working people. In 1906, Joan Trinder's grandfather, William Edward Trinder, opened a shop in Broad Street, Banbury, selling motorcycles and bicycles. Although no longer connected with the family, Trinders toy-shop still trades in Broad Street today.

Chapter Five
Recreation and Pastimes

South Newington, Barford, and Wigginton Flower Show, 1929. Although these events were called flower shows, they covered most garden produce. Typical entries would be:

Potatoes (white kidney)	Prize 1lb of tea.
Apples (culinary)	Prize 2s 6d.
Window plants	First prize 3s, second prize 2s.
Field grasses as a bouquet	Prize 3s.
Cut white flowers	First prize 3s, second prize 2s.
Boiled potatoes	First prize cotton dress, second prize 2s.
Beetroot	Prize 2s 6d.
The best collection of vegetables, 8 varieties, one variety to be 6 different sorts of potatoes of 9 tubers each.	First prize 12s 6d, second prize 7s 6d.

School holidays. Time to explore the fields and spinneys, pick cowslips in the meadow, and catch sticklebacks in a jam jar at the brook. This photograph, taken in the early 1930s, shows the boys with poke caps and girls with hats, one of them hoping she has caught something from the stream.

Camping trip. Girl Guides from Bloxham out on the open road and looking fortunate enough to be getting a helping hand. It looks like a warm evening as the sun is casting long shadows; maybe they are making their way to Broughton Castle to camp. Many Girl Guide and Boy Scout camps took place in the castle fields, encouraged by Lord and Lady Saye and Sele.

The Princess Mary, photographed around the time of World War One. Usually called a traction engine, this mighty showmans road locomotive has its chimney stacked and canvas tied ready to go to the next town fair. The owner, a regular visitor to Oxfordshire fairs, is W. Nichols, amusement contractor, 115 Pevensey Road, Forest Gate.

Harvest festival. Even at a time when religion played a greater part in most people's lives, it would have been difficult to find a more splendid harvest festival display and decorated citadel than this one by the Salvation Army in 1930.

Leafield fête. This photograph, taken in the 1920s, shows what a popular event these annual fêtes were. Apart from a day out for the children, it could have been a fashion parade. A lot of planning and organising went into these events for weeks before the day.

Milton, around 1935. Most children had to make their own amusement during the summer holidays and one of the most popular was dressing up. A favourite with the girls was pretending to get married and, as can be seen, a great deal of care was taken to make it realistic, the parents having been pestered for anything from grannies old things to the lace curtains.

Witney feast fair. The following was written to Mr E.R. Hawkes, 66 Cardigan Street, St Barnabas, Oxford on 15 September 1909. 'Dear Ern, Witney feast fair very dull this year pouring wet Monday enjoyed ourselves in the haunted house Flo Taylor nearly had a fit when we got out just kept her from going right off. Best love from Flo.'

Kingham. The Women's Institute was a way of life, with branches in villages and towns all over the country. They maintained traditional values and kept their standards high. They had market stalls, organised whist drives, and had talks by invited speakers. In many places they were the hub of the social and craft side of life.

Collecting postcards. Until the outbreak of World War One, collecting postcards was a favourite pastime among the working classes as it was inexpensive and a means of keeping in touch. Some of the best collections were created by domestic servants.

POST CARD

THIS SPACE MAY BE USED
FOR COMMUNICATION
IN THE BRITISH ISLES ONLY.
(Post Office Regulation.)

THE ADDRESS ONLY TO BE
WRITTEN HERE.

I. Thought this would do for your collection I got home safe. found all well hope you did. Yours M.

*Miss Allen.
Wells Lodge.
Holkham Park.
Nr Wells.
Norfolk*

Printed in Saxony

Postcard from a friend. The reverse side of this card shows Wroxton Abbey. A domestic servant from the Abbey sent it to her friend, also in service, at Holkham Park in 1906.

Leap-frog. A bright sunny day for a game of leap-frog, but only for the boys. Girls were not allowed and had to play at skipping or hopscotch, that is, of course, unless they were needed to make the numbers up or one was willing to always be jumped over. Then it was agreed, 'We'll let them play then', after all mother had said that nobody was to be left out.

Boy Scouts. Nearly every schoolboy at sometime or another wanted to belong to the local Boy Scout group. It was one of the few organisations that met regularly, provided training, taught skills, and fostered a spirit of comradeship. The photograph shows either first aid training or, more probably as this is the 1915 Scout rally at Chadlington, a team entered into a competition.

Steeple Barton, 1929. Memories and records tell us that folk dancing must have been popular in the county for many generations, and while there has not always been continuity, the art does not seem to have been lost. The maiden in the centre of this group of folk dancers now lives at Horspath and remembers the occasion well.

May Day. Festivities, such as crowning the May Queen and dancing around the maypole, have been with us for generations. There are many variations of the songs and flower arrangements, but what a splendid picture of May Day at Heythrop in 1912.

May Day at Over Norton, 1937. Notice the expressions on the children's faces as they pose for a photograph around the maypole. Seasoned gardeners will tell you that 12 May is the old May Day and the day to plant the kidney-bean seed.

Donkey derby. Between the wars working-class people could not afford seaside holidays, so they had to make the most of local entertainment. Events boasting donkey rides were sure of drawing large crowds. A variation on the donkey ride was the donkey derby, where donkeys were raced to win. Travelling showmen would sometimes supply the donkeys and graze them on the outskirts of the village, usually on the grassy roadside verges. This donkey derby was held in Deddington in 1925.

Souldern club, 1909. Friendly societies were a form of mutual aid for country people, and the club walks held each year were important events in village life. Members would be decorated with flowers and carry banners and poles. Membership came from all walks of life and spanned at least three generations.

The small village of Church Enstone. This photograph of church club day was taken in th summer of 1908. The local band and some of the club members are making their way up th Bicester Road towards the church of St Kenelm. Club days were important events in village life They brought together members of the community as well as providing an opportunity fo clubs to advertise and recruit new members. Considering the size of the village, the event wa clearly well supported. Many generations must have worshipped at the church of St Kenelr since the original church building was erected over 1,000 years ago. The church is unusual i that it has a ninth-century King of Mercia as its patron saint.

The Friendly Society. This Friendly Society gathering of 1912 in the small village of Leafield must have been quite an event. Around 100 ladies are present, so few of the women of the village would have been left out. With the Suffragette Movement making headlines and World War One only two years away, the lives of these women were to change dramatically in the decade that followed.

Chipping Norton. This photographic postcard, taken in 1929, shows local people from Chipping Norton and surrounding villages enjoying the icy conditions caused by the coldest February for more than 30 years. Present-day visitors to the town will be unsuccessful should they try to find Chipping Norton Lake. This is not surprising, since the lake used to be created deliberately for winter recreation by flooding the common land to the west of the town, known as Pool Meadow. Such flooding has not taken place for many years, and today a tree-lined stream and small stone bridge locate the original site.

North Newington youth hostel. During the 1920s and 1930s the advent of affordable private motor cars, and the increase in public transport, changed the way in which people spent their leisure time. Holiday opportunities increased and countless public and private enterprises were created to cater for demand. The Youth Hostels Association for England and Wales was founded in 1930 to foster a love of the countryside by providing hostels and other simple accommodation. The farmhouse hostel at North Newington opened in the spring of 1933, with Mr and Mrs Hutchings as wardens. Accommodation was originally for 10 males and 10 females, with sleeping bags available for hire. The hostel closed in the summer of 1948.

Chipping Norton. The National Children's Home and Orphanage was a voluntary organisation established in 1873 to care for destitute children. A branch of the NCH & O opened in New Street in 1904. The annual fête provided a good source of income for the home, as well as a chance for the children to escape their normally austere and disciplined life. In this scene from the fête of 1917 we see a collection of beautifully made Post Office items for sale, including postcards. Collectors of such items may wish to consider how much that same display would sell for at auction today.

The decorated pram competition. Another scene from the National Children's Home and Orphanage fête of 1917. Notice the band playing in the background.

Family holiday. Car ownership opened up new possibilities for family holidays. Mrs Joan Blann (née Trinder), pictured here with her mother and Aunt, clearly recalls her childhood camping holidays in the early 1930s. The family would drive from Banbury to the Hampshire coast in their Austin 7 and their Morris Minor with a large trailer in tow.

Burford High Street. This sepia photograph was taken outside the Tolsey on meet day. The meet was a regular event, and the huntsman's horn was often heard between November and March. Children were allowed to follow the hunt on foot or by bicycle, as long as they kept quiet and did not get in the way.

Ascott-under-Wychwood football club. This photograph was taken during an era when many people worked in shops, banks, offices, and factories on Saturday mornings. Like today, most towns and villages had a football and cricket team, and the afternoon sporting events brought a welcome end to the working week. Here we see Ascott-under-Wychwood Football Club, winners of the Wychwood League 1927-28. The goalkeeper was Mr H. Clark, and Mr G. Hambidge holds the cup.

Chapter Six
The Effects of War

Claydon. This superb photograph was taken outside Claydon post office in 1914. The Army recruitment poster urges 'Any smart lad' to join the Oxfordshire Light Infantry. Other posters, produced by the Parliamentary Recruiting Committee, appealed to the women of Britain to encourage their men to enlist. Many Oxfordshire men took the 'King's Shilling' in August 1914, helping to bring Britain's total enlistment to an astounding 250,000 within the first five weeks of the war.

NOTHING is to be written on this side except the date and signature of the sender. Sentences not required may be erased. If anything else is added the post card will be destroyed.

[Postage must be prepaid on any letter or post card addressed to the sender of this card.]

I am quite well.

I have been admitted into hospital

{*sick*} *and am going on well.*

{*wounded*} *and hope to be discharged soon.*

I am being sent down to the base.

I have received your { *letter dated* ___ *Aug 19*___

telegram „ ___

parcel „ ___ }

Letter follows at first opportunity.

I have received no letter from you

{*lately.*}

{*for a long time.*}

Signature only } *Jack*

Date ___

(500) Wt. W1566/R1619. 6,000,000. 6/17. H. C. & L., Ltd.

Postcard from the front. An Oxfordshire lad fighting in the trenches during World War One sent this postcard to his sister in Banbury. It was posted from a field post office in France on 20 August 1917. Should the card have fallen into the wrong hands, it would have been of little use since no surname, rank, regiment, or area of battle is shown. It is simply from a soldier somewhere in France.

Oxfordshire soldiers. Old family photograph albums and treasured letters bear witness to the fact that many Oxfordshire men fought in Flanders and the Somme during World War One. These photographic postcards shown were sold in aid of the Blinded Soldiers' Children Fund.

Oxfordshire regiments. Following the declaration of war against Germany on 4 August 1914, the Queen's Own Oxfordshire Hussars, the Oxfordshire and Buckinghamshire Light Infantry, the National Reserve, and Army and Navy Reservists were immediately mobilised. Many young Oxfordshire men were prepared to fight. Born in Milton in 1885, Joseph Henry Bason served with the 11th Hussars as a despatch rider.

Bill Mobley. Born in Banbury in 1900, Thomas William (Bill) Mobley was one of the 2,161 Banburians who served in the forces during World War One. He served with the Army Service Corps in France, and was later posted to Germany with the Rhine Signals Battalion as part of the Allied occupation of the Rhineland. The treaty of Versailles had placed the Rhineland under Allied control and designated it a demilitarised zone, out of bounds to German forces for a maximum term of 15 years. The last Allied detachments left in 1930.

Harry Mobley. Born in Banbury in 1898, George Henry (Harry) Mobley, brother of Bill, served with the Royal Engineers in France as a driver. This photograph was taken to commemorate his receiving a medal for the best-turned out soldier and horse. Harry Mobley was one of the 325 men from Banbury who fell during the war. He is commemorated on a Commonwealth War Graves Commission memorial in the town of Soissons, France. The memorial is mainly dedicated to the British officers and men who were killed during the summer of 1918, when the town fell to Germany. It records nearly 4,000 World War One casualties whose graves are not known.

Red Cross collection. Posted in Chipping Norton in June 1915, this postcard shows Red Cross nurses collecting funds during World War One. Funds collected were used by the International Committee of the Red Cross to provide relief to prisoners of war, and many Red Cross parcels were sent to such prisoners. The two boys at the front look as if they are ready to enlist. Maybe their country called upon them later on in life when once again the world was at war.

Garden hospital. During World War One, various Oxford University buildings were used as part of the Third Southern General Hospital. On 17 August 1914, a meeting of Warden and Fellows of New College Oxford agreed to allow the erection of hospital tents in the college garden for the duration of the war. This postcard shows a few of the many men who were nursed to recovery by hospital staff. Although the hospital itself closed in December 1919, for some of the shell-shocked victims it would be many years before they could come to terms with their experiences in the trenches of the Western Front.

Protection Certificate and Certificate of Identity. This certificate was issued to H.J. Robins on his discharge from the Army in 1919. The postmaster would stamp the bottom of the certificate after receiving a payment of two pounds a week for four weeks. The Army pay then stopped and a job had to be found.

Witney peace celebrations. On Saturday 19 July 1919, peace celebrations were held all over the country. Witney was no exception, and the townspeople worked hard to make the day a memorable occasion. There was a children's procession in the afternoon, and a dinner held for about 250 discharged and demobilised sailors and soldiers in the Corn Exchange in the evening. The photograph, taken prior to the banquet, shows the hall prettily decorated with flags of all nationalities, and the tables adorned with flowers. Over the platform, worked in flowers, are the words, 'Welcome home to our brave boys'. The dinner comprised soup, roast beef and mutton, cherry pies, gooseberry pies, jam tarts, jellies, and blancmanges.

Memorial service, Milton-under-Wychwood. A typical English church with its large stone columns and arches, stained-glass windows, and long wooden pews. Here, and elsewhere, the men who fought for King and Country were remembered. Memorial services took place in churches all over the county, and it is hard today to find a town, village, or hamlet without a war memorial. Forty-two men fell during World War One from the parishes of Milton-under-Wychwood, Bruern and Lyneham.

Fulbrook war memorial. A memorial to the eight men from the village who gave their lives during World War One. The inscription on the front face reads, 'These are the men from Fulbrook who died that we might live. 1914-1918. Faithful unto death.' The fallen are also remembered in a roll of honour displayed in the nearby Norman church of St James the Great.

Chipping Norton War Memorial Hospital. After the end of World War One, it was agreed that a hospital should be built as a war memorial. The hospital could be used by the town and surrounding villages and would do away with the need to travel to Banbury or Oxford for treatment. Funds were raised from donations, subscriptions, collection boxes, and the yearly hospital carnival. The War Memorial Hospital opened in 1920. Of course, patients had to pay for treatment, as this was long before the days of the National Health Service. The photograph shows Lady Margaret Watney opening the maternity ward in 1929.

Select Bibliography

General

Cecil, R. *Life in Edwardian England.* Batsford, London (1969).

May, T. *Agriculture and Rural Society in Britain 1846-1914.* Arnold, London (1973).

Mingay, G.E. *Rural Life in Victorian England.* Heinemann, London (1977).

Royle, E. *Modern Britain – A Social History 1750-1985.* Arnold, London (1987).

Terraine, J. *Impacts of War 1914-1918.* Hutchinson, London (1970).

Oxfordshire

Jessup, M. *A History of Oxfordshire.* Phillimore, Chichester (1975).

Ward Lock Red Guide *The Cotswolds.* Ward Lock (1970).

Williams, E. C. *Companion into Oxfordshire.* Methuen, London (1935).

Penguin Guides *Berks & Oxon.* Penguin Books, London (1950).

The Victoria History of the County of Oxford. Oxford University Press, Oxford.

Bloxham, C. *Portrait of Oxfordshire.* Robert Hale, London (1982).

Oxfordshire Town & Village Index

ND - #0225 - 270225 - C0 - 246/189/6 - PB - 9781780914855 - Gloss Lamination